# Taking the F Train

## *Also by Linda Lerner*

*City Girl* (Vergin Press, 1990)

*No One's People* (New Spirit Press, 1992)

*She's Back* (Ye Olde Fonte Shoppe, 1996)

*New & Selected Poems* (Ye Olde Font Shoppe, 1997)

*Anyime Blues* (Ye Olde Font Shoppe, 1999)

*No Earthly Sense Gets it Right* (Lummox Press, 2001)

*Greatest Hits 1989—2002* (Pudding House Publications, 2002)

*A Koan for Samsara* (Ibbetson Street Press, 2003)

*The Bowery and Other Poems* (March Street Press, 2004)

*Because You Can't I Will* (Pudding House Publications, 2005)

*City Woman* (March Street Press, 2006)

*Living in Dangerous Times* (Pressa Press, 2007)

*Something is Burning in Brooklyn* (Iniquity Press / Vendetta Books, 2009)

*Ding Dong the Bell, Pussy in the Well* (Lummox Press, 2014)

*Takes Guts and Years Sometimes: New and Selected* (NYQ Books, 2011)

*Yes, the Ducks Were Real* (NYQ Books, 2015)

*A Dance Around the Cauldron* (Lummox Press, 2017)

*When Death is a Red Balloon* (Lummox Press, 2019)

# Taking the F Train

Linda Lerner

The New York Quarterly Foundation, Inc.
Beacon, New York

NYQ Books™ is an imprint of The New York Quarterly Foundation, Inc.

The New York Quarterly Foundation, Inc.
P. O. Box 470
Beacon, NY 12508

www.nyq.org

First Edition

Set in New Baskerville

Layout and Design by Raymond P. Hammond

Cover art by Angela Mark

Library of Congress Control Number:  2021945289

ISBN:  978-1-63045-079-3

# Taking the F Train

# ACKNOWLEDGMENTS

Grateful acknowledgments are made to the following journals in which these poems first appeared:

"The Wild West Comes East on Citibank Bikes" in *Lummox 3;* "I Could Have Been in New England" and "The Road Back to Yemen from a Brooklyn Laundromat Goes Up in Smoke" in *New Verse News;* "One Daylight Saving Hour" in *Forever Night (Siempre Noche): The Alternative New Year's Day Spoken Word / Performance Extravaganza - 2017 Anthology;* "Coyote Promptings" in *BoogCity;* "The Same Age" in *SoFloPoJo;* "Those Mourning the Coney Islands of Childhood" and "The Invasion" appeared in *Yes, the Ducks Were Real* (NYQ Books, 2015); "The Day Before" in *Misfit Magazine;* "A Dead-End Path" in *Waymark,* #3 & 4; "Endangered" in *Maintenant;* "Brooklyn Ruins" in *The Brooklyn Voice;* "Waiting For the D Train," "Playing with Tense," and "That Place" in *Gargoyle;* "If Only," "Upgrade," "Skinning an Elephant," and "The First Time of Anything" in *Chiron Review;* "Find the Source" in *Paterson Literary Review;* "As Big As A Hairline Crack" in *Red Fez;* "The Power of a Dime" in *Lummox 6;* "On Seeing the Georgia O'Keeffe Exhibit…" in *The Opiate magazine;* "A Little Sorry" in *Like Light,* an anthology edited by Bertha Rogers; "The Lone Ranger Rides Again" in *From Somewhere to Nowhere: the End of the American Dream (The Unbearables Anthology;* "Rats" in *The Café Review;* "The Butterfly Effect" in *Trailer Park Quarterly;* "The 'To Have and Have Not' Years" and "Maximum Security" in *Poetry Bay Presents: Poems & Illuminations;* "Like a Prayer" in *Free State Review;* "Taking the F Train" in *Home Planet News;* "A Cover- up" in *Lummox 9.* The eight poems included in sections 5. Aftermath and 6. Pandemic 2020 were previously included in the chapbook, *"When Death is a Red Balloon"* (Lummox Press, 2019).

*In memory of Lowell Scheiner*

*and 40 years of unconditional friendship-love*

# CONTENTS

## 1. The Crossroads

## 2. Taking the F Train

## 3. Mishaps

## 4. Left Unfinished

## 5. Aftermath

## 6. Pandemic 2020

# Taking the F Train

# 1. The Crossroads

# The Wild West Comes East on Citibank Bikes

*A Former New York City Mayor's Legacy*

I jump out of the way as
they come speeding out of the virtual world
wind-blown sun dappled winding in
and out of traffic into heart-stopping danger

when I first saw those bikes corralled in stalls
throughout the city I imagined horses,
the awful smell of horseshit
on the street, not the sanitized version of
another era's get-a-way for

anyone to jump on
pay at one of the many stations afterwards
and return to a cyber safe house;

if along the way someone gets knocked down, hurt
a few keep riding as though nothing happened
others stop, bewildered, when an ambulance is called
and...couldn't be...they were in their proper lanes

or when

a truck door flies open smacking a biker
on the head, blood gushes out, and
the border marking two worlds blurs;
the man taken to a hospital, stitched up, and released
doesn't quite know which side he's on
how he got so lost, why or
what he needed to break out from

# That Nay…Do You Hear It?

maybe it was the outlaw thing had me
posing on a motorcycle I'd never ridden
who'd never even learned to balance on a bike
imagining a tale I told of riding down
a winding road by a cliff's edge in New Mexico
when I'd been safe in a car, someone else driving
the outlaw thing caged, photographed
to be retouched…

One day I saw a pony behind a fence
and wanted to jump on…when
I approached with my intention,
I got the loudest nay

It's that nay I've never stopped hearing;
when I jump on the wrong horse not
meant for me to ride, don't
jump on any horse, play it safe
avoid the big fences, decisions
to jump or turn back, riding toward
love toward aging, toward…

the nay heard decades before when I told someone
"Josephine called me," to explain why I crossed in
the middle of the street, tried to outrun a car

the nay heard every time I ride for acceptance
start playing games with that damn horse
on the page or off, doesn't matter; what does:
ignoring the one waiting patiently for
me to jump on and just go…fence after fence

# Maximum Security

They watched a horse who stumbled
as a colt, now push death out of the way
and run as if he could do it forever,
his name drew people like a drug:
guarantees strewn about like bones
from another era, they invented
new ones fast as that horse
jumped hurdles others missed
smoke filled drunken lives stumbled,
unprotected, diseases they got
inoculated against, but for chance
a misstep, bike a woman didn't see
leaving a restaurant, suddenly
knocked out of life
a puddle this thoroughbred
jumped over, forcing him
off track, disqualified
at the finishing line

## The Lone Ranger Rides Again

when the leader of the new free world
the lone survivor of warring factions
came out shooting, guns in both hands
he was at his golf club, having just sent the ball
flying to the other side of the fence bordered his land
his whole country, as reports of
missiles he ordered fired warnings to someone
in retaliation for…only it was
gunpowder filled the air he breathed, and a horse
he rode in the back of his chauffeured limo
his head filling with plans for a high enough fence to keep out
all those bad hombres he'll rope up like cattle
and send flying back over the fence which
kept growing like those knock down drag out fights
he'll have with anyone from anywhere who opposes him,
images over flowing so fast into his daily
reports no one could keep track of who or
how many there were or where he was, a masked man
riding into yesterday when a man was a man
and women, ah yes women…along with
a staff of shift shaping Tonto sidekicks
he'll bring back the great promise of frontier life

# The Crossroads

I think of it now as the old city
glimpsed thru cracks
the way an old self sometimes
breaks thru without warning
brought back by those
painted naked ladies buying what
people want them to sell
pretending they don't; sometimes
I imagine what it would be like
to sneak back there, be one of them
be who I was for a while
disobedient always in trouble who
didn't fit in and didn't pretend to
if I could be that naked-alive again
*needs to learn the hard way* someone once said…
pushing my way through crowds down streets whose
stores brag name brands and the latest technology,
spot Elmo and the Cookie Monster
looking like cartoons of outlaws
Columbia University street wannabes
once studied mentored by Herbert Hunke
hitting up a group of tourists
in a cash for photo hustle
*something must be done about this*
a voice cries out rushing by, and
*oh look, there's one of those ladies*
heads turning to catch a quick look
fast as it once took to snatch
a gold chain from someone's neck
to take back home with them

# One Daylight Saving Hour

I am testing its limits
reaching back through time zone years
to see how much can be crammed
into a single daylight hour, saved
in a space no bigger than
my first Manhattan apartment:
I take what I need, people give me
make what doesn't go together, fit;
look ma, no hands, I cry riding my first bike
riding words across a blue-lined grade school notebook
so fast I couldn't stop, riding with my first man
on a creaking bed in hot Mexico City
out of breath in a future he didn't
belong in & someone else quietly
slipped out of in the middle of us:
it is an hour like the universe
continually expanding that I want to give
to another, show him how much
can be packed inside, never been
good with numbers, I try to get him
to forget about logic, just feel
where my words are headed

# Coyote Promptings

that trickster my old lover from last century is back:

>    my nerves pick up his scent
>    and I'm cheering him on as

he eludes capture running down the streets of New York
through lower Manhattan crossing city & state lines
into Queens, New Jersey, defying authority once again
forcing people to leave their digital sanctums
>                *catch me   catch me*
on 9<sup>th</sup> Avenue or is he now on 23<sup>rd</sup> Street, the same coyote
roaming through our backyards
>                        *catch me catch me if you can*
sounds in their gut & they're off:

I can feel him messing with my mind again
as he tugs at my memory and think
I'm too old to start this again,
knowing it's a lie, that even after
all these years it wouldn't take much…
and knowing that is knowing
all I need to know…

# The Day Before

*For Donna Kerness*

an unlikely New York City calm
takes hold of me in Los Angeles on landing
raining so hard the day I left and
not knowing though fearing what never happened
marvel at what did

flooding worries, the rest, gone
bridges and roads to them temporarily blocked
as in a storm, so unexpected

a friend from San Antonio writes
about one still a way from where she lives
but close enough...
flood waters keep rising, she writes, homes drifting
out of lives, a place where someone loses someone forever;
I've never been to Texas, but I've been to that place
and know, this day, any day, could be
the day before Texas

# The Freeway

I'm a New Yorker not a westerner
land is scarce where I come from
and I am not used to this freeway
I find myself stuck on with a man
I barely know who offered to be my guide
telling me how well he's done
to explain why he didn't make it
and what he could have done differently
which makes no difference now;
an accident up ahead, he says…
cars are veering from one lane to another
so close, doesn't look like I'll make it anywhere,
says his wife is an accountant who
comes from my part of the country
he visits once or twice a year
suggests eating at his house rather than going out
before driving me to my next event when
a car cuts too close to ours
he makes a sharp right to get out of the way
barely missing another car, asks
if I'm in a relationship noting how long
it's been since…I check to make sure
my seat belt is secured, and lie to get off that path
he's already left, saying
they have it made, referring to
a couple of Hollywood stars he knows

# The Butterfly Effect

been 18 years he said, since
you've been back, noting how long
didn't compute its actual distance...
I had no clue, couldn't wait to board that Delta plane;

back meant when I could still
walk those Haight Ashbury streets pretending
to be that young hippie chick I never was;
meant before 9/11, before I heard him say that
on returning from Viet Nam, he knew that
was there, this was here, clearly marked, separate
was before someone at a ticket window asked,
senior? and felt myself teetering on an edge
was before I packed three chargers
that would connect me to what
I wanted to escape from, wouldn't let me forget
who I was, allow me to play with time

I walked the familiar San Francisco streets
everything looked the same, only something didn't feel right;
I didn't get any warnings like the man
time tripping back millions of years in a Bradbury story*
told to stay on a path raised several inches above the ground
how stepping on a single blade of grass
could affect the future...

* "A Sound of Thunder" by Ray Bradbury

24

# The Shifting Ground

after my college boyfriend joined
the open road club, on a day he and
a few others picked me up in
a hearse they rented to carry
their hiking gear, my mother's
expression emitting seismic shock
waves that drove me rushing us out
fast as I could, never thought that
I who just went along for the ride
or because I was crazy in love and
didn't want him alone with another
female doing what I wasn't ready for
that one day from a height of several
decades I'd be looking down at
a fractured fault line running through
my life, hear a gravelly sound
struggling to get back to where
it had been, and I no longer could
hear what I took for granted then

# The "To Have and to Have Not" Years

reminded of that time I smoked
cigarettes and tried to sound like
Bacall, walked around the house repeating,
"You know how to whistle don't you,"
to a Bogart I've yet to meet; wanted
nothing more than to sound like her
on a stage

as I listen to old audio tapes of
myself and try to yank my voice out
of whatever morass it has gotten stuck in
over the years, wanting nothing more
now, than to sound like that woman
in those tapes

# I Could Have Been in New England

*For Nina Howes*

   my father's voice that I hadn't heard
since he died interrupts a news report
about anti-Semitic crimes increasing
here, *didn't I warn you*, he says
the smoke from 70-year-old explosions in Russia
rises up from bomb threats at Jewish centers now
and I'm fighting with him again to
stop living in the past, *that's over with*
I say, but as the newscaster
continues citing threats across
the country I begin marching
back to my college years protesting
discrimination against blacks
signing petitions against segregation
do it from the safety of my birthright;
   *there's nothing to worry about*, I tell him
   *it's not us, it's Muslims who have to worry*
   *who need our help today…*

outside the sun is shining; in the warm
winter light everything looks as it always has;
a friend is telling me about her trip to Germany
to where the death camps are now tourist sites;
as she walked around the city, went into shops
visited a park, watched children playing,
their parents looking on, relaxed,
said, *I could have been in New England*

# Find the Source

*April 19–28, 2019*

a friend says of ants that just appeared
in my kitchen like live bits of worry;
unable to, I place traps everywhere.
This week Easter & Passover merged
people send *have a happy* to which ever
I ignore, nothing about Passover
I don't observe, but doesn't feel quite right
to say, like saying I didn't love my father,
unable to trace back to exactly when
I knew   he didn't love me

the ants, one step ahead of me, are now
crawling on my desk, over my computer
across a photo of a family seated at a Seder
fast uploading those I sat through as a child,
my divorced uncle, a perennial
looking bored as my brother asked why
and why again, nothing about why
we need bitter herbs to remind us of
ancient difficulties, plenty now, I think,
trying to block what finds
new ways to get in;

…my friend writes, "the ants eat the bait,
go back & feed it to the queen and
they both die," comes through old hurts, regrets
my brother's, *why is this night different from
all other nights**

*a reference to the four questions asked during a Seder

# The Poet, like a Bird on a Wire

*from Leonard Cohen's song, "Bird on a Wire"*

is trying to decide whether to use **a** or **the**
as in a free woman or the free woman
contemplating the risks and
feeling like that stunt man who
danced across a wire between
the twin towers
110 stories above death
knows **a** could be anyone of hundreds
not even remotely her, but
**the** solves distance, something she
might be able to navigate but
expose her songs of freedom
for the lies that inside truth—

the stunt man kept up his dance
across the wire for an hour
she's been at this an entire day
days in fact trying to move down the line
when it snaps and sends her
falling thru the poem
to where the towers once stood

# The Same Age

a woman struck by the sight of a badly bruised
mud-faced child on the New York Times' front page
before me, didn't say anything right away,
a kid who looked like he might have been
in a bad accident, maybe bullied, or abused,
heard stories about this sort of thing happening
all the time, a child who didn't fit in like
someone she once knew from her school days
a boy pushed face down into the ground
his eye swollen beneath which dried blood
rorschached trauma…what's in the news sometimes
gets tangled up with what happened in one's own life,
what one sees and doesn't do anything about
went unlanguaged in her mind which I heard by
how she stared at this picture, and then
somewhat embarrassed as though she'd been caught
said that she didn't have her glasses with her and
asked me if it was about….

        I read the caption to her: "a five-year-old
rescued after an airstrike in Aleppo, Syria," without waiting to hear
what she was going to say; the where & what didn't
seem to matter, said she hoped he'd be all right
that someone would help him; *my son is
the same age*, she added, *five*, and
held him closer as she left the coffee shop

## The Road Back to Yemen from a Brooklyn Laundromat Goes Up in Smoke

*separate*, he asks, as he puts my laundry
on the scale. *Yes, separate*, I say
*still*…week after week, tries to make
this American woman understand
what it feels like, no, make me smell
the smoke of mortar & rocket fire politics
keeping him from getting his wife & daughter
everything so carefully arranged, end of
June, his graduation from college, and then…*puff*
*do you see?*
            what I see is the road
twisting and turning in his mind
teasing him *now it's here, now it's gone*
of a promised cease-fire;

when he speaks of his birth country
of things getting worse
I see frightened people imprisoned
in their homes being deprived of basic necessities

I see a country being raped…
I do not see his wife and daughter
he will not let me

## A Morning in May

I never learned to swim and
when as an adult, I tried, did it to please a man
the water wouldn't hold me up,
I believed it as I believed that avoiding
water would keep me from drowning....

It's a morning in May, rainy cool and
I just opened my eyes, feel good
and begin to turn on the day:
news, gossip, apocalyptic warnings:
important everything is important

by noon I'm fighting to stay on
top of it, like jumping waves

I've watched people do at the beach,
what my mother said could sweep you away
never said to where, now drag me
into a partly submerged future:
it's either swim or drown...

there are days that won't let me turn them off

# Instructions from a Yoga Teacher

*Remember to breathe*

It's the remember that trips me up every time
I spread out my mat to begin my
downward/upward dog day...someone says
jump, I do to get through everyday all day

and forget to remember...
a website once asked me to sign something
to prove I'm not a robot

*breathe in when you rise, out when you go down*
*in when you do this, out when that,* he repeats

doesn't work, I can't get them in sync,
and even if I could how can I prove that...

just this morning in my local café
I started to order the usual
scrambled on the side, & lightly buttered
the cook knew the moment he saw me
nodded, and turned away

*longer on the exhale, he says*

forcing me back here...

I can't stretch out my breath
that far, don't tell him, but he hears
and hears how much I need to let out

*follow the breath,* he answers, *follow the breath*

might as well have said
follow the yellow brick road, the yellow brick road

I mimic to myself, take a few short
stumbling out of breath attempts

and feel like I'm on that cracked, crumbling road
Alice started off on to the Emerald City with
the wizard to guide her home

I am not Alice, not trying to get home
which never really was, & is gone now, anyway

the only wizard is this instructor, hardly a wizard
he'd admit himself, nudging me with every breath,
to remember

# Upgrade

being three or four systems behind meant
my Mac couldn't be upgraded, I was told,
and alerts will keep teasing me about
where I couldn't go, which felt like exiting
the R train onto 8th Street, now just
another street, not the bohemian road
that led onto European-style cafes, exotic Indian shops
jazz venues, and bookstores I'd get lost in
pretending I didn't have to take
the train back to where I am now

unable to go forward in one world and
back in another, hearing Dylan's
    *The Times They Are a-Changin'*
in my head, while struggling to open a birthday card
with an outdated flash drive I couldn't upgrade

just as I can't advance from how I feel
to my numerical age and keep on ignoring
undercurrent alerts telling me, it's time...it's time

a friend suggested I call the Geek Squad;
for the computer, I asked?
what else, she said, incredulous.

that's the problem, I said
what else...

## Endangered

I'm on a crowded NYC subway, can't see who
a man is talking to or catch a single word
but violence in his voice sounds too close,
I run out at the next station, into another car
breathing a sigh of relief when

I hear the sound of glass breaking
every few minutes in a woman's voice
the man she's with mistakes for laughter,
sees only a warm, beachy smile
he'd like to lie down on, mouths words
I can't make out from all the noise;
they're leaning against the door
facing me and I'm thinking, she's crazy;
keeps on for 15 or 20 minutes when
they get out and

two teenage boys rush on, loud voices
speeding on skateboards jump between
cars and vanish too fast for it register;
nobody looks up from their cell phones.

I get off the train thinking,
I haven't heard a single word
since I got on. Since he's gone
and they now come filtered
through noise flatlined
on a screen.

# 2. Taking the F Train

# Taking the F Train

### 1.

long before I knew there was an F train, I heard it
rumbling through our three-room apartment
the moment my father got home from work.
Every night he took it to the end of the line,
my mother silently beside him as it made
local stops at every grievance he had
starting with a country whose promises
teased him out of Russia into one failed
business venture after another, managers
whose voices whipped down so fast—
he'd seen horses treated better—
the cost of each complaint carefully
weighed, how much to support a wife
and two kids—
the cost of being alive: last stop.

In the morning he got up and
took the BMT to work. Nobody
in those old Brooklyn neighborhoods
could afford to take the F train during the day.
Poor, working class, immigrants living
rent controlled lives someone else owned.

### 2.

The first F train I was on ran silently
along the same line as my father's;
I didn't know it when I said
*I'd never,* packed my bags and moved
near the only subway close by

passed my own give 'em hell stops
on those unmapped stations between
East Broadway & Delancey, 2nd Avenue.
& Broadway-Lafayette, the train crawling along
except when it didn't: the conductor
announces signal problems: I'm stuck
telling someone off over & over until

### 3.

the train starts to move again,
I get to my stop, and begin my, *that's OK*
to those when it isn't
the 9–5 every day all day, *that's OK,* till
I'm back on the F train, a scared teenager

a woman no longer ignoring
a man's hand beneath me in a movie theatre
a co-worker's unwanted hand
someone's *watch it* finger pointed at me
I point away, those *it's for your own good*
words, I ignore, my father's,
you just can't do whatever you like in life
I throw back at him

### 4.

and keep going on and off
the same F train that jerks me around
every weekend, sometimes with a big D, E or
M on it to throw me off, or doesn't come at all
forcing me to take an A to the J
find where it's rerouted by whatever
circuitous path, take it and that's
when everything becomes NOT OK and

### 5.

I'm riding past where my father's train stopped;
to get where I want to go, I don't get off
and get there just in time every time

"Thank God for the F Train"*

*By Ben Sidran (From the album, *Picture Him Happy,* released Jan. 17, 2017)

# The First Time of Anything

*A British astronaut, Tim Peake, at an outer space station, accidentally misdials a woman, asking, "is this planet Earth?" taken as a hoax.*
—The Telegraph

Calendars begin arriving months before
like subway preachers…
*He's coming,* one yells out on an A train,
*When? October. 25th* a voice answers;
he could have said January. 1st, as
expectations mount for what
everyone's been waiting for:
not me. A non-believer,

I want an old new year
one that fell out of the sky
like a meteorite, wasn't programed,
the first-time gravity didn't hold me down
and I flew on words, on music
in a ballet class, first time
undressed past skin I flew out
of my body in a man's arms,
stood up naked before a crowd
not caring what anyone thought,
the day my sick cat showed me what
being a mother feels like

each time I flew off the planet
I was raised on, a new year

## Thunder

it slipped under our conversation next day
not ever reaching a crescendo, even trying,
a prolonged undertone heard as I lay in bed and
waited for that crack, the kind that
happens when he'd say, I want a divorce
or there's someone else only he doesn't say it
pauses between them were like breaths, in which we
…but there's wasn't any we
I was alone last night listening for
what I hear when we stop talking or start
that constant rumble in the background
seemed as if it would just go on & on
like quarrels with our parents and
ourselves…lasted maybe half an hour
or a little more
next day I asked him, *Did you hear it?*
*What, thunder?* he asked. *I heard nothing*
It is a beautiful sunny day outside
we're sitting in an outdoor café
and I still hear it so clearly

## The Word, Wife

because of how I was with him
like someone who's been there a long time
they assumed I was his wife; I didn't contradict them
maybe he didn't hear that word, and later when
he must have, also let it go, easier
not to mix it in with talk of why we were there
so it stayed outside, lingered in the air like that other matter
of his heart, what the pictures showed & didn't
I brought him some coffee while we waited
remembered milk & sugar, but forgot a stirrer
to mix it in; he threw out the coffee;
outside some sharp words when I couldn't
…doesn't matter what

except I recalled why long ago I vowed
never to be called wife….

## Changing Colors

She tries to tell him something he can't hear
*What if it happened in other places,* she asks
when he tells her to get out of her office more
A *blue glass paper weight is now*
*yellow,* she says, when she took it out
of the box, *and a greenish enamel flower pot*
*is trailing off into brown; but still green, right?* he asks
she doesn't answer him.

He's standing behind a wall of primary colors
strong light hurts his eyes and he can't
see what it's doing to the colors
the gray his wife favors wearing, whiter now
the alley ways between them
down where she's been slipping

when she thought he didn't notice
what he suspected but knew
about the danger of straying off
well-traveled mental roads

*I can smell the earth seeping through*
*the flower pot,* she told him, *and the yellow*
*now smells like spring rain*

                  *and then*
he didn't want to hear any more

                  *and then*
but to lure her safely back to
where nothing ever changed color

## A Dead-End Path

she might have been hurling rocks from a cliff
words flew with such blunt force... *don't turn around,* he said...
scattered about the subway station entrance
                                    a safe distance behind us

across from where we were seated
a loud metallic clatter... *no one but you turned around*
knives, forks, hundreds of kitchen utensils spilled out
of a large bin the waiter carried
bounced off each other into our conversation
hitting the restaurant floor   *I'm not everyone,* I said
                                    there was no safe distance

they kept falling out of the bin
out of her mouth   *into her cell phone* I said
*no, that last one was aimed at you   don't look*
he said, too late...all that beautiful
sunny day-after-day-blue deepening into
blue sky week right through my birthday

a perfect weather storm raged between
words uttered and those that weren't

# Thank You, You're Welcome

struggling to open my umbrella I didn't hear
a woman repeat what I saw in her coal burning eyes as
she shoved past me, *In NY you always keep moving,*
and felt like I'm on one of those moving walkways at the airport as
we headed to the restaurant past a long line-up of
people pushing to get into Macy's,
does anyone ever say *Excuse me* anymore
anyone from past Thanksgiving years hurrying
its dead through as we sit down to eat
and the man I am with begins talking of retirement
starts to make plans for when…and after
I begin attacking a plate piled high with stuffed turkey
candied yams cranberry sauce
he's talking about maybe this June or next
I'm thinking about ordering some pumpkin pie
he says, maybe I'll start a blog, my late lover
makes a quick comeback on his computer
the waiter asks if we want anything else,
he shakes his head and hands him a credit card
I hold up my cup for a refill my parents' ghostly voices
fill with unsolved quarrels…I have an urge to say,
*you're not excused* to anyone
and keep moving

# The Loudest Argument I Ever Heard

began before they even entered an uptown F train
a man & woman, late 30's early 40's stood
by the door for a few minutes without moving—
I've never touched hot coal but think
I know what it would feel like from
the look in their eyes;
someone seated next to me got up and left
she took the seat; he kept leaning against the door
his hands loud, full of rage
slammed down on a kitchen table that
suddenly sprang up in the aisle between them
hers flew at him one after another
I saw dishes break, hundreds of recriminations
their eyes lock...no, bolt...against everyone else
who acted as if nothing...
the man's hands rammed down years dredging up
what hers threw right back at him
fingers made small incremental movements up a long list
his hand sent scattering,
before I got off
I could swear I heard a baby crying, smelled alcohol
saw an apartment trashed, a couple intent
on hurting each other as much as love is capable of

## A Little Sorry

I ease myself into the day
to avoid another flare up
like those arguments we had left over from
the night before that could send me
flying out of my skin,
comes out in bursts now which I calm
down with a little sorry, but not
too much...it's my life, my body
to do with as I wish, but a little sorry
that I pretended everything is fine
pushed fast through angry words
you no longer can speak
I heard from every joint and nerve
as I ran down the stairs to do what
I always do, only nothing is as always, you and
my younger self remind me

# Blame

## I.

a woman I never met is banging
on invisible bars to be let out,
*I hear it in her eyes,* her daughter says
for me to hear it too,
a voice silenced by feeding tubes
and a ventilator

…words only take me so far,
and in truth, I don't want to go
any further than this…I think
about soldiers being taken prisoner
in Iraq or Afghanistan, countries
I've never been to, people put in dark
cells, no idea if they will ever get out
goes on sometimes for years
far from where I am

## II.

who is to blame
for taking a woman's life
to prolong it? And have.
The doctor who gave her a year
to live without a new heart valve
the daughter who told them
to go ahead…the woman who
saw the new door open and walked
through it past her 86 years,
just yesterday she'd wrapped days like scarfs
around her, so many she couldn't choose,
breathing in sun like air, confident
there'd be more days now
like these

### III.

one long day stretches over weeks
the forecast unchanged:

*Do you want to live,* her daughter asks,
a hoarse voice hauled out by sheer force of will,
*Live,* she begs her daughter, no, pleads with her
who misunderstands; a matter of semantics
the banging keeps on, louder now

# As Big as a Hairline Crack

Sometimes it comes from behind and you don't see it. Maybe later, unable to move past the pain from a broken pelvis, an 80 something year old former dancer saw the irony.

The first time I was nine & a half, running to get away from the nagging, quarrelsome atmosphere at home. I ran around the corner to join a group of girls playing across the street. I saw the car coming I tried to beat; I saw the girl on the skateboard, decades later, I ran around to avoid hitting. Or being hit.

the injured woman's daughter told me that her mother was out taking a walk. She was too vain to use a cane, and often used a shopping cart instead. It was a lovely day, and she was feeling good, heading toward the senior center where she taught yoga classes. Suddenly, a few women began screaming at a man in a wheelchair; he kept crying, "I didn't mean to hurt her, I don't know what happened, it's my eyes...the sun's glare...I didn't see..."

I didn't see the man who would hurt me in the eyes of the one who loved me. I didn't want to see how far beneath the skin his wedding ring had penetrated; didn't see that removing it was really irrelevant. That the word ex is a verbal placebo.

It's like bones broken, displaced in a hand or foot or that conversation which took a wrong turn one day; swerving too fast around what we tried to avoid, landed us in the wrong place which we sought to mend with various kinds of sorry. You can't even see where it was broken, the doctor said of my finger. "There's stiffness that's always there," I said. "I feel it more strongly on waking." He nodded.

Pain caused by a hairline crack in her mother's pelvis, took away the pain of needing a wheelchair, my friend told me. "Maybe just till it heals and I'm back," her mother said. Her daughter never asked how far back she meant.

## The Door

It's the door that doesn't get slammed
the one in your mouth you hold back
behind clenched teeth…
he doesn't mean to be cruel
is just proud, maybe bragging a bit
of what a young woman wants to give him
it has nothing to do with you
an old friend he's having dinner with
you feel the door pressing against your teeth
struggle to keep it from breaking out and
when you push it far enough back
slide off the conversation into
the safety of U.S. air strikes in Iraq & Syria
the possibility of retaliation here he picks up
your lead, sensing something isn't quite right
but sensing the danger follows you
into this temporary shelter

## On Seeing the Georgia O'Keeffe Exhibit at the Brooklyn Museum

*May 30<sup>th</sup>, 2017*

"a curse" she called that door
stuck in a crumbling adobe wall
even bought the house to get it
and still....

not my problem, and I didn't come here
to hit a wall, but I did
tried to get past what "the men" as
she called them said she painted
the men who saw vaginas everywhere
lies they said of her
oriental poppies, calla lilies,
red canna, I tried to dismiss

but in a black flower I'd never seen before
an eternal flame burned at its core:
a flower I kept staring at
black as the door she struggled
for years to take off the wall

## Travelling Down the Pacific Coast Highway with David Hockney

I wanted to bite into that luscious orange
could feel his buttery yellow melt
in my mouth, tasted the green cool as celery
twisting road I've never been on with
a man who excited me in quite this way
crossed gender lines and
it didn't matter that he prefers men sexually
when he got in his car he drove me
right off that cliff

# Painting Apples

*After Reading Two Stories by George Saunders*

her mind runs blindfolded down a very long street
past her dead parents, friends from grade school,
no separation between blocks and nothing to make her stop
she runs past herself sitting at her easel painting apples
a real artist now, not going to be one like she is
running down that street...painting apples that
look so real, her little brother wants to grab one
and bite into it, the only person in her family who
is doing well because of her, well one bad turn
she runs past now and turns it around, her own child-
brother she raised, nobody could take from her
runs past her art teacher boyfriend who said she had
to get past painting apples, but this is her canvass...
so tired of running, if only there were marked lines
like on those streets where she played hopscotch and
jumped over them, jumping so fast, as she did sitting at her easel
just like her heart jumped when she saw him
happened so fast...busy trying to bring those
apples to the forefront, she didn't hear him knock
then did and opened the door without asking who...
he looked so much like her brother
so lost, she asked him in before she saw the knife
partially held behind his back, wanted to turn him
around, way she just did with her brother, or did
that happen a long time ago, maybe even something
she was going to do, hard to tell on this
sidewalk that has no separation, past & present
jammed together with the future and
this boy who stood there looking so lost
holding up his knife asking her for...

## Taxi Dancer

it was 10 cents a dance and being spun
around the 30s so fast she barely kept her balance,
doesn't her daughter understand, this
thing she struggles with now is nothing…
a woman who'd worn skin off her bones in
cheap dance halls and chorus lines
who had enough girl in her long past youth
to make men open their wallets—
a man is supposed to pay she lessons her…
a cane is out of the question
she said, flinging it across the room

the floor tilts…she grabs hold of a shopping cart
stands up straight as she can and a dime-a-dance girl
positions herself for her next number;

I've seen those women but never really saw them before
stooped over carts they push through every kind of weather,
a loaf of bread or a few small items thrown in as a decoy
carts that never get filled, pushing them as
they once pushed baby carriages, brooms
and vacuum cleaners across marriage floors
to clean up a husband's dirt, women sprouting up
from urban cracks, pushing through laws
that said a woman couldn't do this or that
one breath following another
across a century…

# Think Crocus, Think Heart

snow narrows the sidewalk
the cold pushes you further inside
you didn't know there was any further
but you're there; the snow hardens and
you wonder how long it will take to crack it;
shovels are no use; people try something
that looks like a pitchfork, small teeth
at the end; some say a sword is what's needed
you wonder how much warmth
it will take to melt a small hole
for you to take it in as through a straw
let it infuse your whole being
to imagine the first crocus breaking through
not question whether it's the earth or
your heart, just let it come like the
first flush of love, when you were
ready to burst out of your skin and
expand the sidewalks of the world
to dance down

# 3. Mishaps

# Heated Plastic like Heated Words

It was one of those black plastic trays
with dividers for food I brought home
from a take-out mid-eastern restaurant, ate what I wanted
refrigerated the rest and heated it up in the stove next day when
my cat began sniffing around me rather loudly and
an awful smell like tar filled the room
the fire alarm went off
I ran around opening windows,

wasn't thinking, as we don't when we say
words we try to clean up next day with
other words like I did when I tossed out all
his vodka bottles one night and the words
hardened into a permanency nothing could remove
I pretended weren't there, but couldn't now when
smoke was visible in every room

I waited for the stove to cool down, took out
the disfigured tray, partially melted onto the stove
and wire rack, tried to scrape the melted plastic off
the rack which was hardening as I worked and couldn't be budged
nor would it come off the stove

"Don't you know that plastic turns to metal when heated?"
he asked, exasperated, the one whom I depend on
when things go wrong, one who is always right,
*don't you know...*

followed by a lecture of when he toured plastic factories
for a magazine, detailing what happens when plastic
when words when a heart is burned too often

# A Can Partially Opened / A Heart Partially Closed...

too much grime on an old can opener
way past cleaning I replaced with one
that broke apart a quarter of the way through,
same length of time it took to close my heart
to someone I don't recall opening it
up to in the first place; that was before
he broke down into pixels for a nanosecond
in the middle of telling me...
I kept the old can opener that still worked
and purchased another one
*Should have bought a good one in the first place,*
he noted, who must have sneaked inside my heart
decades ago while I was lying inside
someone else's and took it for granted;
partway through, that can opener also fell apart,
I tried to put the parts together mixed up
the openers they belonged to while being
overly helpful or not enough to him who
insisted he was fine, just trying to
regain his balance, wouldn't let me come
in too far, something about the apartment
and *it's just a bruise,* he said, *will go away*
told me to stop trying to save money
and get something that works;
I've given up struggling to fix what's broken
clean up what's settled in too deep
took his advice and got a can opener
that finally works; I make sure not to let
anything unsavory accumulate on it

## What Hasn't Started Yet Had Already Begun

it began when he tried to learn the cause
of his difficulties, same as when I bought
a new toaster, recommended in Yelp reviews
and burnt the toast that things went haywire;
I let it cool off and marked the bagel setting:
no better luck...he saw another expert from
the list of best in New York, without things improving
sought out a third and told something slightly
different from what the other two said who
didn't quite agree but didn't disagree either;
I brought the toaster back, a sale item
it couldn't be returned, a make no one
reported having trouble with and was asked
if I really followed the instructions, told to
try again, give it time, the expert told him,
things sometimes get worse before...
he could rush home to tear up that list
see me throw the toaster out front
a signed marked *free* on it:
if someone asked what was wrong,
we'd tell them it was the settings
the diagnosis, way to figure it out,
smoke rising up from the toaster
the experts listed in the best in New York
the smell of something burning
we couldn't get rid of, and no one
who knew how to put out a fire
that hadn't started yet

## The Power of a Dime

I hate clichés, imagine it's what a musician hears
when someone strikes a wrong note,
so, when someone on TV commented
how life can turn on a dime after getting bad news
from a doctor, I cringed,
only the dime won't go away this summer,
it is hovering over all of us, circling the globe
when suddenly without warning
there's never any warning...

It's that dime that's the lie I've been telling others
refusing to say the word stroke, it's his back,
he'll be fine I say, to keep the truth from myself,
that what happened to him will go away, we'll go
on as if everything that isn't the same
and hasn't been for some time before, is
because to admit that is to admit this

# Brooklyn Ruins

### I.

I know ruins when I see them
doesn't have to be centuries old
like the Parthenon or Acropolis,
it's the sense of something crumbling around me
every few blocks huge cranes are
lifting out the soul of my city…
another newsstand, a small grocery store
candy shop vanishes…I cross the street to avoid
being squeezed into a makeshift walkway
and end up going through several
blocks away, forced to walk beneath
towering machines which at any moment could…but
don't this time and thank construction workers for
guiding me safely out of danger into another kind.

### II.

A few blocks away. A few blocks from my home.
A luxury high rise is going up not far from
a half century old grocery store. The man
behind the counter who might be the owner
is speaking Italian to an elderly man.
A couple of gray-haired women, stooped over
loaves of bread on shelves stocked with
familiar name brands squint trying to read the price;
a few kids are mulling around the candy stand,
the owner gives credit doesn't ask
which card writes down the amount on a piece of paper.
The woman on line before me doesn't ask how much.
*How do you know the amount?* I asked her.
*He knows,* she said.

I don't understand Italian and the store doesn't always
have an item I want but in this cold season
it feels like a splash of warm sun.

### III.

Re-zoning begun by a former mayor works its way
through the city like a tape worm lifting roof tops
off future buildings; real estate developers in bidding wars
throw a few promised affordable apartments
onto waiting lists; those told they earn too much or
too little for what isn't available yet
pack up adding another subway stop
to their commute and keep moving toward
the end of the line the sound of the ocean's roar
the fear of drowning...

### IV.

Artists whose vision stretched canvasses into
dangerous areas made safe get
rents hiked beyond their means, resize
imaginations to fit smaller & smaller
work spaces now doubling as apartments.

A painting of an amputee lies beneath the sign,
Brooklyn Works. First one arm, then another
then the legs...four images. The painting isn't signed.
Everyone knows who did it.

Manhattan moves down town into Brooklyn
Brooklyn moves into Astoria & Flushing.

## V.

The sound of jackhammers breaking ground
follows me home. I remember to
look behind me when walking down
a deserted street, make sure
I'm not being followed
walk faster and shut the front door
tightly behind me.

Only how fast is fast enough? Where are the locks
to keep out greed?

# Waiting for the D Train

*On receiving a late-night phone call from a friend on a train station*

Every alphabet labeled train she's ever taken from the Bronx, Queens
is crammed into that D train she's been waiting a half hour for
to get home...blame it on night track work, economics
and bad decisions brought her to the end of the line
this is the borough of Brooklyn she moved to not the cool city
*place to be*, whose outsourced name
advertisements sold her

this is the borough in which I was born, a three room tenement
neighbors quarreling voices heard through the dumbwaiter
housewives sitting on stoops complaining, crying kids
tugging at their nerves, never enough money enough anything,

the borough in which I rode the same D train from Flatbush
to Brighton Beach dreaming of the city whose
bright light promises pierced the skies of my imagination
didn't resemble the 4<sup>th</sup> floor poorly heated walkup
I could afford looking out on other walkups...

*a lot of Russians live in my building* she tells me, and
I think of my Russian born father dreaming
of an America he'd live in for decades without
ever really seeing that country as he bagged groceries
after businesses he started failed

*and a lot of Chinese take-out places,* she said, same
as where she last lived, but no cafes, no bookstores
interesting small shops, or those quiet brownstone blocks
she'd seen which had a different feel to them
...that other Brooklyn whose name led her to

this borough as a young girl I couldn't wait to leave and
didn't have the heart to tell her

# The Invasion

I think it's just another morning rush hour
on the F train, day before Thanksgiving and
lighter than usual, got a rare seat
not far from a middle-aged balding man
muttering something I barely take note of when
I hear warnings about Mexicans
not paying taxes, stealing our jobs,
refusing to learn English, thousands of
Mexicans coming on this train followed by
Dominicans who are no different and
should be sent back to where they came from—
doesn't see me or anyone but those immigrants,
hasn't forgotten about the Chinese either
like the Mexicans and Dominicans who
keep entering his country, this subway car,
nobody stopping them, and this poor man,
an American citizen, doesn't he have any rights,
soon he won't be able to read his paper
the Daily News will be written entirely in Spanish,
only one more stop, I can't wait to get off
when the Russians jump on, who've already
taken Coney Island from us, what next
the train pulls into Jay Street
and I squeeze out through a crowd of
unruly Mexicans piling on
followed by Dominicans and....

# Those Mourning the Coney Island of Childhood

baffle me; I start to follow someone on his roller coaster squeals
and slip off into heated arguments blanketed on
hot sand stretching out the length of
my father's two-week vacation I jumped waves
in rough ocean waters to escape from,
hauled back by my mother's fears I'd be pulled out
too far and was years later when
in a skimpy bikini let the sun
bring out all the heat I had teasing
the boy lying beside me who said,
"Let's go beneath the boardwalk…"

sand seeped into ice cream melting days
mustard-smeared hot dogs and cotton candy
that looked better than it tasted
as I walked up & down the wooden planked boardwalk
with friends wondering where all
those cute boys we saw now, were, back then

the sun, always too strong for my fair skin
followed me to other beaches and deeper burns
decades from that Coney Island of my youth
whose wooden planked boardwalk is being replaced
the Ferris wheel with a big wonder wheel
and new shops charging outrageous prices;
I haven't been back, but they say
the ancient cyclone still roars loud as ever

# The Bugs Get In Anyway

hot sticky days spent
squashing bugs that got in
through half screens
some so tiny I never saw
what bit me, others

my computer caught
through the spam blocker,
cousins I hadn't seen since childhood
retired early from 9–5 proletariat worlds
circle the globe in mobile homes
                                    flying
after vice presidents of the American dream
their Republican children became / some

bump up against my *lead a different life*
keeps me from becoming
the *poor relation* my mother was…
blood lines link us from her two sisters and brother
petty quarrel jealousies split apart

cousin Allen's compliment flip flops:
"Poetry doesn't sell," I tell him…
"You were the lone free spirit of the family—"
his words evoke my Russian father's ghost
and this wayward daughter he said Kaddish for

who Americanized the foreigner
who embarrassed her, this man
whose daughter I now boast of being:

*I needed you then…I don't need you now*

Allen sends me a photo of himself
his father smiles right through
daring me not to see him;

there's no full screens for
these old brownstone windows
whose two panes don't quite fit...
I stuff the space between them with towels
to keep out the bugs
who get in anyway

# Skinning an Elephant

It's that elephant Orwell fired shot after shot into
that same elephant who lay dying, not dead
the natives rushed to with baskets and
stripped to bone in less time than it took for him to die

same elephant I keep seeing in the frantic search
to pull out every scrap of memory, every photo taken
with someone suddenly gone: a fierce competition
to show their relationship went back further
was deeper that they were the first to have known

what they missed seeing then...I too
no less than the others...

it's not the elephant I see now
it's his skeleton

# Rats

The rats are out, a woman said.
I just saw one behind the gate;
there was an article about
rats in this park and around here,
the other woman said. I know, I joined in;
my friend's door man said that he
had to close the door at night
because the rats were trying to
get in; people blamed construction
going on down the block.
That was a long time ago.
Well, they're here now, the woman
said; I considered moving further away
from the garbage disposal can.
Early evening was also feeding time
for mosquitoes. The two women
got up and left. I didn't want
to go back home yet. It was hot,
my apartment stuffy, and about now
they'd be sneaking out of holes
in the 6:00 news…. When I was
growing up in Brooklyn people spoke
about rats where they worked; it seemed
everyone had one. My father's rat was
a man named Joe Cohen. That name
kept coming up in his evening rants
to my mother, I saw talk of rats in movies
about the Mafia. Someone spoke of
a sign warning people of rat poison
in an area I passed every day.
There was some confusion when a person
mentioned the increasing prevalence
of rats here, and I thought they were
referring to people. Once when I
complained of roaches an exterminator
told me to plug up all the holes, that

they can get into the smallest space.
Rats, too, I thought. I've seen them
hovering around sabbatical holes
in one college where I taught, and
lurking in words like congratulations.
If rats can get into anything,
how would I know if they found a way
to get inside me?

Once I met
the wife of a man I was having
an affair with, and the way she
looked at me, was the way
that other woman just looked
when she spoke of seeing a rat...
that was a long time ago

# 4. Left Unfinished

## I Want Out Loud

to hear a voice so I can feel its words
breathing down on me, not
bloodless text conversations
so, when your voice escaped
through the copper cable wires of
last century's hospital phone
I lit up: yours lost in the accident,
you complained about
the nurses, cardboard-tasting food
uncomfortable bed, each complaint
leading me deeper into the word
back to the Caribbean Island
you visited as a young man
with your first ex, to the
golf course where you last
played with your late buddy
to a job you loved for over
20 years and without ever deviating
from that list of complaints,
your voice led me to the
edge of mortality's precipice

## Two Trips

headed toward one place I didn't want to go to
when the plane lifted off for the other;
an hour ahead fell behind; when we landed
I wasn't sure which trip I was on
having prepared for southwest heat
not the other kind: my skin burning
in the 105-degree day's thoughts of
him, those tests he took, and fears
as I walked down San Antonio's streets
got lost & would learn that to lose
my way here is not really being lost.
*Find the Alamo,* someone said, *And
you'll know how to get back...* I did
for nearly four decades, but how
to a place I don't recall being in
before someone who isn't my lover
and is more than a friend, who
pulled me back from edges I didn't even
know I was on...

# Left Unfinished

bad writing you'd say of
that seven-hour long sentence
you ran silently by me in the hospital,

a trick you had
to leave off writing in mid-sentence
for something to complete the next day,
worked you said
                    so I'm waiting
like a child who puts a tooth under her pillow
for the tooth fairy to get and leave
something in its place, I keep busy

sometimes grab a day
out of the wrong tense, lift a piece
of memory and play with the facts
to right a few wrongs

the grammarian & journalist would
not have approved, the man who
didn't know, just how much,
would have understood

# Just Sand

A woman is walking alone by the East River. I watch her from where I am sitting several feet away. Mid-July, a steamy month except for this fall-like cool day. One of the ten best, someone I loved would have said. You'd agree. Hate hot weather…better than very cold, I always added —a running discourse we have. The woman is walking very slowly, one bag flung over her shoulder, another, larger one, over the other one. She notes two cops talking a few benches away, keeps them in her peripheral vision, and continues to walk at the same leisurely pace.

I am not fooled by this seeming calm, more like sleepwalking. She suddenly stops, looks across the river toward the World Trade Center, reaches into the larger bag, and flings out a handful of something over the railing before I can catch what it is. This happens a few more times.

The distance between us keeps growing shorter, though I haven't moved. She walks faster now as though diverted from what she hadn't planned on doing. It's such a perfect weather day. If I can find the right words, I'll bottle it for you to keep. I don't know how long I've been sitting here, watching her, before she reaches her destination, stops and looks out at the Brooklyn Bridge; I am right there beside her now. Directly behind it is the River Café, where you took me on my birthday, remember? She digs into her bag and, like before, flings out a handful of something. Does it again. And again. A mother and child are standing nearby, watching her. "When my sister died," the mother said, "we scattered her ashes in Coney Island."

The boy turns around and says, "That's not ashes. It's just sand, Mommy."

Now, indistinguishable from the woman's pixilated image breaking up over the East River.

I get up and start walking away. Maybe later or tomorrow, I'll visit you.

# A Leafy Sunday October Morning

it's a drizzly gray inside/out kind of day
doesn't really matter where I am
but better here to get through what
once was our day: the park, mostly
empty except for a few kids playing,
watchful parents close, a couple
with a dog seated on the next bench,
an elderly man walks back and forth
airing grievances I can't catch but
hear him clearly, moments of
other Sundays, quick flashes
as before a migraine a child's ball
breaks through, a parent's *Sorry*,
my *That's OK*, and for a few minutes is,
I bite into a bagel, let coffee break through
when a park attendant with a loud
leaf blowing machine sweeps
leaves into small groups to garbage
until the area is mostly cleared;
looks wrong, I think, emptied of
what life even dead leaves bring,
wrong, as when toward the end he said,
"It almost doesn't seem worth it,"
a life gone with speed of light
into a single pronoun: wrong
to clear out everything

# Every Sunday for Two Years

I asked if he wanted coffee and a bagel
or donut along with the NY Times
if he had enough milk
needed sugar, if he had
something for dinner that night
I asked about the book he was
working on with a man whose
grammar drove him crazy
if he wanted me to pick up
something at the post office
get him a book from Barnes & Noble
or a DVD he wanted to watch

I never asked if he needed something
he couldn't ask for

he never asked how I'd feel afterwards
not giving it to him

# Gone

a big white dog materialized as I exited
the elevator onto my friend's hallway floor,
transformed by the dimly lit space into a spectral being
held me in his gaze, pacing back and forth
outside his door seemed to be hovering
between two worlds as for weeks that man had;
I don't know how long I stood watching that dog
watch me, only that he'd vanished when
hours later I left, having told my friend about
it said that he must belong to the people next door;
I never saw that dog again, or the person my friend
once was, and whom I knew would never see again

## When Death Is a Red Balloon

Scared shitless last week when I
came to your room, saw you asleep
and kept calling your name
pulling your hand, *Wake up*, I shouted
until you opened your eyes...

Oh, I tried again, sat by your bed for hours
holding your hand, sending my voice like a rope
to where you lay several levels below sleep

love, which never made it into word,
flowed through my touch with the meds from IVs
that kept you breathing

and then I saw that red balloon
like those in comics, instead of words,
a wire scrawl of hieroglyphics,
once there, wouldn't go away

I didn't want to see it hovering
near you, but I did; how you'd hate it,
*It's not funny*, you'd say, blaming me
for what I couldn't control

I watched the air slowly being let out.
Three hours passed and I left...it was just before...

the balloon is gone now
you are asleep, I am by your bedside
once again, holding your hand

if you can hear me, I must tell you
there is nothing I can ever imagine experiencing
more horrible than watching the air go out
of that balloon

# Playing with Tense

*written immediately on waking, April 7, 2019*

It's early April; I'm telling him about
a play I saw in the fall, *The Lifespan of a Fact*,
I thought he would have liked.
*Maybe they'll revive it*, I say, though
it's not likely, but…he looks hopeful.
I am, too. There's more color in his face, and
he seems strong enough and ready
to get out of his wheelchair, to continue
from where he was a few years ago.
The weather is getting warmer;
maybe he'll be able to go down
to the Brooklyn Heights promenade
where we often liked to walk.
I don't bring up the business of those ashes
I threw into the East River in July.
It has nothing to do with him.  He
agrees. I just focus on the present,
now that he got better from death.

# 5. Aftermath

# A Bad Weather Time

stone cold, I say
you think I'm talking about
the weather which I am
when you ask, what it's like outside
would ask if you could, as
last winter when housebound;
snow could soften these days
like that powdery stuff we
used to get in New York,
remember? Wouldn't do anything now,
don't have to say it, I hear you,
a few promising flurries
feels more like those *Sorry
for your loss* words I kept hearing
afterwards, fake weather, you'd say...
when the cold gets to be too much
I close my eyes and grab hold of your hand
as that last day and don't let go
till I feel the weather changing...
that's the past, you always said,
whenever I....

# Very Warm for May*

If April is the cruelest month, May is the falsest
with its fake-looking warmth; *It's so cold*, I said,
as we headed down the street one sunny
morning last May, and recalled
his mentioning an old Broadway musical,
*Very Warm for May*, I'd never heard of;
now, would never forget

I wasn't thinking of how much time
we had left, but what this unseasonable
weather meant for the planet, and

how convenient an excuse,
made me seem so much better,
than I am, so less self-involved.

Two months later, I couldn't hide
the truth from myself: right then,
I wasn't thinking about the planet
at all: only what it meant for me

*Jerome Kern & Oscar Hammerstein, 1939

# Like a Prayer

Something about his, "I like your shoes,"
after I read something sad
because that's the way it's been since
*It will get easier,* words last July
struck me as funny, and why today,
not quite a year later, grateful that
no one had used the word, closure,
I even wore those red beaded moccasins
which had no support, weren't comfortable
*Thank you,* I said to this man I barely knew
trying hard to suppress a laugh
I couldn't hold back any longer
as more and more people began to stare
at my shoes and I slipped away

# Where Is Here?

*For Andrew & Lowell*

You both would have hated this overpriced café
I wondered in to cool off and write
on a very muggy Sat. afternoon—
mostly millennials asking for almond milk
for their coffee, ordering food like avocado toast,
a few parents with kids being ignored,
even those who technically can't be
called millennials—
you would have looked around
and walked out even before seeing
the saleswoman thrown off when
I handed her cash for an iced something
instead of a card; so, what am I doing
sitting here scribbling in a yellow note pad
people look at askance…except
maybe that's the point; you both
are now gone, I am here
alone trying to find out
where exactly here is for me now

# 6. Pandemic 2020

# A Cover-up

when a large horse stumbled
in Central Park and collapsed,
news spread of his inhumane treatment
to all of us, stumbling in uncertainty;
no way to explain what couldn't happen
is happening; political weather
grew more turbulent, warnings
about everything descended

and when I just about had enough
fever and a hacking cough put a stop
to it; for three weeks I was inoculated,
nothing could touch me.

Until that horse. Feeling better
meant I could smell him now
this horse I never even saw, learned
had shown signs of distress
before collapsing, a struggle to cover up
put him out of the way fast
keep people from seeing:
what we feared afterwards
had nothing to do with a horse.
And couldn't be euthanized so easily.

# A Sunny Corona March 26<sup>th</sup>, 2020

Jolted by a song that comes on*
as I'm searching the web for
items store shelves are emptied of
brings you back cursing as we
rush through horn-blaring jammed streets
a neon-lit sun flashing every
color of the spectrum around
the clock—

five minutes before the curtain went up,
the last time we went to the theatre and
I saw New York in those two decades
after the attack on the World Trade Center
before it looked like an abandoned movie lot,
a few lone individuals, sad-eyed smile
in passing, tourists in their hometown
my city, brought down a second time;

If Paris is a lady, New York is an old warrior
called back once again to summon
all its youthful strength, to rise up
in fiery magnificence
from the ashes of defeat,
      reborn

*reference to "The Last Time I Saw Paris" by Jerome Kern

# How It Is

A masked man comes to the door
I see him from the peephole
go out and quickly hand him
a large green bag, *Tomorrow*, I say,
he nods, no other words
I rush back inside

A neighbor opens her door a crack
shaking her head. I motion
*What choice do I have,*
she shrugs and shuts her door.

The streets are quiet, a few people
walk hurriedly by, armed with fear.
Fights break out in people's eyes
who get too close, back off
in time. Sometimes not.

We don't see bullets strike us
any blood, so we keep on
until we can't, become one of
the missing.

*have you heard from—*
someone says, *no, you...not on fb*
*maybe he's just taking*
*a break...I heard the same*
*about...stop, you know better*
we all do, and keep going, eyes averted

till we're safe at home watching
people being massacred in
another country; it was like that
at first. The fourth wall in tact
before our death broke it

# That Place, April 2020

I call it that place because there is only one right now. Maybe it was after a tornado hit somewhere in the South, or that fire which kept burning up more and more of Los Angeles last year, flooding in New Orleans when the levees didn't hold, earthquakes and tsunamis in Japan, Haiti, California, Indonesia—images that coalesce into one: piles of debris where there were homes, a neighborhood, a city, people wandering through them searching for what didn't happen.

I think of our planet now. We don't see the debris; we see a pile up of numbers, streets nearly emptied, stores boarded up, a few people searching in what once was.

I think of Pompeii wiped out by a volcanic eruption. An entire city covered in ash for centuries before it was found; I think of this place slowly vanishing, so slowly we don't notice, some ignore, until....and even then....and even now as over a million deaths announce it, wait to go back to what was when we were heading toward it.

CPSIA information can be obtained
at www.ICGtesting.com
Printed in the USA
BVHW030858061021
618259BV00006B/205